Piano Music

"Prole do Bebê" 1,
"Danças Características Africanas"
and Other Works

Heitor Villa-Lobos

DOVER PUBLICATIONS, INC.

Mineola, New York

Bibliographical Note

This Dover edition, first published in 1996, is a new compilation of thirty-three piano pieces originally published separately in authoritative editions, n.d. The Dover edition adds a composite table of contents, headings in English and Portuguese, a glossary of Portuguese and French terms used in the music and typographically unified main tempo markings throughout. The music for piano four hands, pp. 122–137, which was mispaginated in the original edition, has been put in correct "secondo"/"primo" order.

English translations of the original Portuguese headings and performance notes have been specially prepared for this edition by Stanley Appelbaum. We are grateful to Ms. Jacqueline Donado, a translator for the Brazilian Consulate, New York City, for providing updated Portuguese spellings and accents in the table of contents and the glossary.

International Standard Book Number: 0-486-29384-X

Manufactured in the United States of America
Dover Publications, Inc., 31 East 2nd Street, Mineola, N.Y. 11501

CONTENTS

GLOSSARY OF PORTUGUESE AND FRENCH TERMS IN THE MUSIC

a fora, prominent, bring out
alegre, festive, joyous

baixo, bass
bem fora (o canto), (the melody) very prominent
bem marcado o canto da mão esquerda, the left-hand melody *molto marcato*

(le) chant [Fr.], (the) melody
chanté [Fr.], sung
com elegância, with elegance
com espressão irônica, with an ironic expression
com muita alegria, with great joy
com muita graça, very gracefully
com muita simplicidade, with great simplicity

en de[s]hors [Fr.], distant
en rhythme [Fr.], in rhythm

𝆑 o canto, the melody loud
forte o canto da mão esquerda, the left-hand melody *forte*

giogoso [jocoso] = *giocoso*

joyeux et animé [Fr.], joyous and lively
justo = *giusto*

ligeiro e saltitante, light and hopping

m.e. [*mão esquerda*], left hand
modéré [Fr.], moderate
muito = *molto*
muito destacado = *molto staccato*
muito leve a mão direita, the right hand is to play very lightly
mystérieux [Fr.], mysterious

o baixo sempre bem marcado, the bass part always *ben marcato*
o canto a (bem) fora, the melody (very) prominent
o canto bem ligado, the melody *ben legato*
o mesmo mov^to por ♩, the same tempo per ♩ [♩ = ♩]

plus modéré [Fr.], more moderate
pouco a pouco = *poco a poco*

retenu [Fr.], held back
rijo e sonoro, firm and sonorous

sempre muito subtil [sutil] a mão direita, the right-hand melody very subtle throughout
sinal [also *signal*], marking

très lent et très expressif [Fr.], very slow and very expressive

um pouco grandeoso = *un poco grandioso*

vagaroso, slow, deliberate
vago e independente, freely moving and independent
vague [Fr.], indistinct
vif [Fr.], quick, animated

Second Suite for Children

Segunda suíte infantil (1913)

1.

2.

From Second Suite for Children (1913)

3.

From Second Suite for Children (1913)

Allegretto

Bem marcado o canto da mão esquerda

Tempo 1º meno

rall.

poco rall.

4.

From Second Suite for Children (1913)

Allegro non troppo

African Folk Dances

Danças características Africanas

Rags

Farrapos

Native Dance *(Dança indígena)*
No. 1 (Op. 47, 1914)

To Ernani Braga

Kankukus

Native Dance No. 2 (Op. 57, 1915)
from African Folk Dances

To Nininha Velloso Guérra

Kankikis

Native Dance No. 3 (Op. 65, 1915)
from African Folk Dances

Floral Suite

Suíte floral

Idyll in the Hammock

Idílio na rêde

No. 1 (Op. 97, 1917) of the suite

Rocking motion [Acalanto]

A Country Girl Fond of Singing...

Uma camponesa cantadeira...

No. 2 (1916) of the Floral Suite

Garden Party

(Impressions of a Festivity of Vegetable Gardeners)

Alegria na horta (Impressões de uma festa dos hortelões)

No. 3 (1918) of the Floral Suite

Poco animato ["pouco animado"]

The Baby's Family

Prole do bebê (Vol. 1, 1918)

Little Light-skinned Girl

(The Porcelain Doll)

Branquinha (A boneca de louça)

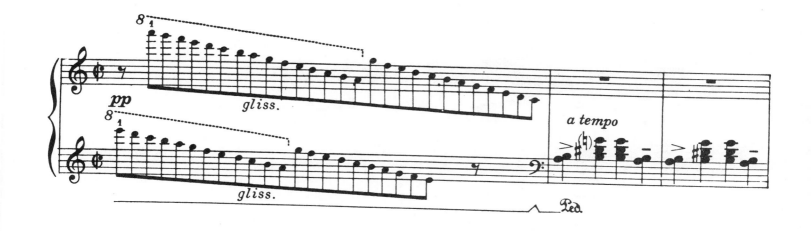

Little Dark-skinned Girl

(The Papier-mâché Doll)

Moreninha (A boneca de massa)

No. 2 of The Baby's Family (Vol. 1, 1918)

Animato molto marcato

52   The Baby's Family

Little Mestizo Girl

(The Clay Doll)

Caboclinha (A boneca de barro)

No. 3 of The Baby's Family (Vol. 1, 1918)

56   The Baby's Family

Little Mulatto Girl

(The Rubber Doll)

Mulatinha (A boneca de borracha)

No. 4 of The Baby's Family (Vol. 1, 1918)

Little Black Girl

(The Wooden Doll)

Negrinha (A boneca de pau)

No. 5 of The Baby's Family (Vol. 1, 1918)

The Little Poor Girl

(The Rag Doll)

A pobrezinha (A boneca de trapo)

No. 6 of The Baby's Family (Vol. 1, 1918)

Punch

O Polichinelo

No. 7 of The Baby's Family (Vol. 1, 1918)

Witch

(The Cloth Doll)

Bruxa (A boneca de pano)

No. 8 of The Baby's Family (Vol. 1, 1918)

Simple Compilation

Simples coletânea (1918)

Mystic Waltz

Valsa mística

No. 1 of the suite

In an Enchanted Cradle

Num berço encantado

Moderato [Modéré]

Rolling

(After the poem by Albert Samain)

Rodante

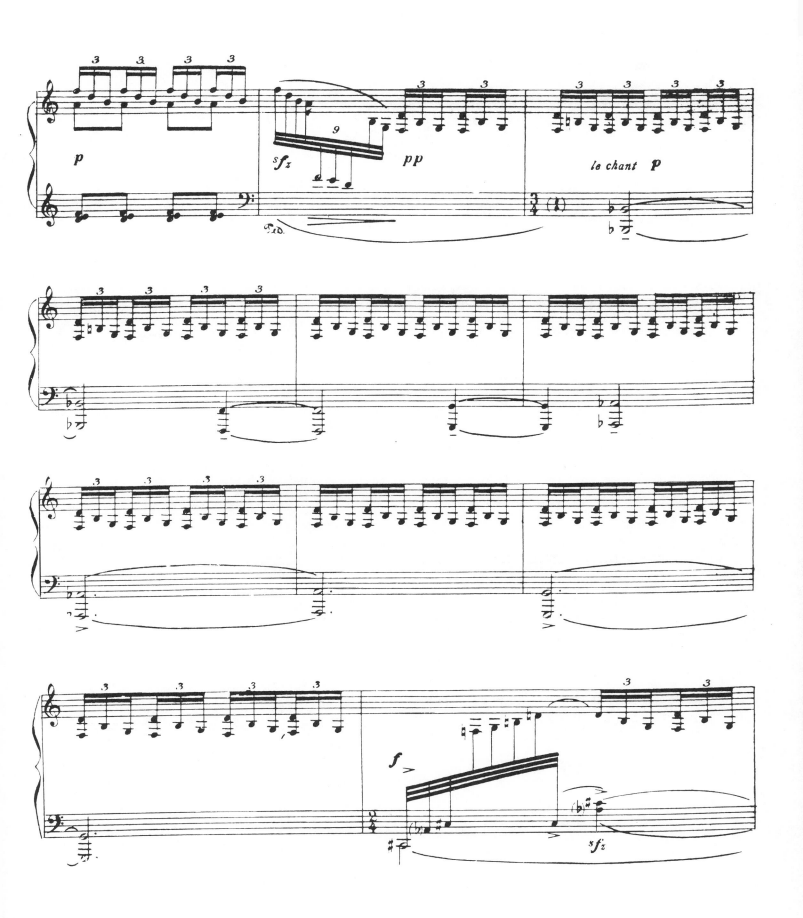

Fairy Tales

Histórias da carochinha (1919)

To Nylzóta

In the Enchanted Palace

No palácio encantado

Movimento di minuetto [Mov^{to} minuetto]

To Ahygarita
The Courtesy of the Little Prince
A cortesia do principezinho

Quasi movimento di gavotta
[Qusi mov^{to} de gavotte]

No. 2 of Fairy Tales (1919)

To Russinha
And the Shepherd Boy Was Singing

E o pastorzinho cantava

Andantino espressivo

No. 3 of Fairy Tales (1919)

To Kilzota

And the Little Princess Was Dancing

E a princezinha dançava

No. 4 of Fairy Tales (1919)

Tempo di gavotta

To my nephews

Children's Carnival

Carnaval das crianças

The Little Pierrot's Pony

O ginête do pierrozinho

Edited by Barrozo Netto

Allegro grazioso e ben ritmato

The Little Devil's Whip

O chicote do diabinho

No. 2 (1919) of Children's Carnival

Pierrette's Ruse

A manha da pierrete

Edited by Barrozo Netto

No. 3 (1919) of Children's Carnival

Allegretto poco capriccioso [?] ["capriccietto"]

The Little Domino's Jingle Bells

Os guizos do dominozinho

Edited by Barrozo Netto

No. 4 (1919) of Children's Carnival

The Little Ragpicker's Adventures

As peripécias do trapeirozinho

No. 5 (1919) of Children's Carnival

The Coquette's Mischievousness

As traquinices do mascarado mignon

Edited by Barrozo Netto

The Fife of a Precocious Daydreamer

A gaita de um precoce fantasiado

Edited by Barrozo Netto

No. 7 (1919) of Children's Carnival

The Gaiety of a Children's Band

A folia de um bloco infantil

No. 8 (1919) of Children's Carnival

In the Composer's Original Scoring
For Piano Four Hands

The Gaiety of a Children's Band

A folia de um bloco infantil

For Piano Four Hands *(a 4 mãos)*   **SECONDO**   No. 8 (1919) of Children's Carnival

Moderato, tempo di marcia, accelerando [accelerado]

The Gaiety of a Children's Band

A folia de um bloco infantil

For Piano Four Hands *(a 4 mãos)* **PRIMO** No. 8 (1919) of Children's Carnival

Moderato, tempo di marcia, accelerando [accelerado]

124   Children's Carnival

PRIMO

SECONDO

PRIMO

SECONDO

SECONDO

SECONDO

PRIMO

SECONDO

136   Children's Carnival

PRIMO

END OF EDITION